Let's Have a Tea Party!

EMILIE BARNES

with SUE JUNKER

HARVEST HOUSE PUBLISHERS
Eugene, Oregon

Let's Have a Tea Party!

Copyright © 1997 by Emilie Barnes and Sue Junker
Published by Harvest House Publishers
Eugene, OR 97402

Indigo Gate
1 Pegasus Drive
Colts Neck, NJ 07722
(732) 577-9333

Design and Production: Garborg Design Works, Minneapolis, MN

Library of Congress Cataloging-in-Publication Data
Barnes, Emilie.
    Let's have a tea party! / Emilie Barnes with Sue Junker.
        p.   cm.
    Includes index.
    Summary: Provides instructions for creating several different tea parties, with themes like a family tea, a garden tea party, and a musical tea party. Includes recipes, decorating ideas, games, and activities.
    ISBN 1-56507-679-6
    1. Afternoon teas—Juvenile literature. 2. Children's parties—Juvenile literature. 3. Cookery, American—Juvenile literature. 4. Menus—Juvenile literature. [1. Afternoon teas. 2. Parties. 3. Cookery.]   I. Junker, Sue.   II. Title
TX736.B373   1997
641.5'3—dc21
97-8362
                                   CIP
                                   AC

Printed in the United States of America.

99 00 01 02 03 04 05 06 / **IP** / 10 9 8 7 6 5 4

CONTENTS

Please Come to Tea!

I'm Emilie Marie, and I want to invite you to tea! A tea party is one of my most favorite things! I love the food, the games, the special decorations, and the chance to be with my friends. A tea party is always a fun time of being with people I love.

For a long, long time—since long before cars and telephones and computers—tea has been served between 4:00 and 6:00 in the afternoon, and it still is today. A tea party can be very simple—just sharing a cup of tea and something sweet to eat with a friend. Or a tea party can be very fancy— lots of friends wearing their dressiest clothes and using pretty china and cloth napkins. You can have a tea to celebrate a birthday, a special holiday, or a good report card! Or tea can be just because! There's always time for tea!

Teatime Treats

One of the best parts of a tea party is what goes with the tea! Usually special little sandwiches and yummy sweets are served. Tea sandwiches are tiny sandwiches made with very thinly sliced bread, which is cut into special shapes. Let me tell you how to make them. First spread a thin coat of butter, mayonnaise, or cream cheese on the bread to keep the sandwiches from getting soggy. Next add the filling. People usually think of cucumber sandwiches when they think of afternoon tea, but you can make whatever kind of sandwiches you want.

Once you've added the filling, cut the sandwiches into squares, triangles, long strips, or fun shapes. Tea sandwiches are easier to cut if you chill them first. So wrap your sandwiches in a slightly damp kitchen towel and then in wax paper before you put them in the refrigerator.

One neat thing about tea sandwiches is you always get to cut off the crusts. So, when you're ready and an adult is watching, trim the crusts with a serrated knife (the kind of knife that has teeth). Then cut the sandwiches into shapes. You can use that same knife, but sometimes I like to use cookie cutters to make special shapes.

Along with tea sandwiches, you can serve cakes of all kinds. Sometimes they're extra small, too, and then they're called "petit fours." And don't forget to include whatever fresh fruit is in season!

One more thing. You can serve any drink you want at a tea party—apple juice, hot chocolate, chilled lemonade—but be sure to serve it in pretty teacups. If you do want to serve tea, you have lots of flavors to choose from. Have fun trying different ones at different parties!

How to Make a Cup of Tea

Making tea is easy, but you may need an adult to help you. First fill a teakettle with fresh water and set it on the stove to boil. While you wait, run hot water from the faucet into your teapot to warm it up. Pour the hot water out of the teapot and add your tea bags. Use two to three bags for every four people. As soon as the water in the kettle has started boiling, take the kettle off the stove. Let the kettle rest for a minute so the hot water will pour more easily. Then pour the water over the tea bags. Wait five minutes. Now your tea is ready to pour for your guests.

A Garden Tea Party

Little Mr. Buzzy Bee,
Gather honey for my tea;
Come into my garden, do,
I've every kind of flower for you.

I love the garden in our backyard. It's one of my favorite places to be. I love to lie on my back in the soft, cool grass and watch the fluffy clouds float by, smell the sweet air, and listen to the wind dance with the leaves. The roses and gladiolas are always so pretty. Sometimes a hummingbird will visit, and I usually spot a few tiny white butterflies that my grandma calls "skippers." And the little table out there is a nice place to read a book, sit and think, visit with a friend, or have tea!

So please step outside with me for a special garden tea.

Invitations

Invite your friends to your garden with a bright yellow sun or colorful flower invitation. Fold a white or light-colored piece of paper in half. Draw your design so that the top part touches the fold. Then cut out your design but don't cut through the fold. Next color the front of the invitation, then write the important details inside—the date, time, place, and your name. You might also give your phone number and ask your friends to

1
FOLD

2
FOLD

3
FOLD

RSVP (that stands for "répondez s'il vous plait" and means, in French, "please let me know if you can come"). Be sure to say it's an outdoor celebration and let your guests know what to wear.

An Outside Table

Cover a picnic table or patio table with a bright flowered sheet or a colorful tablecloth. A table with an umbrella can be especially pretty. You can decorate edges of the umbrella with garlands of ivy and wind a vine around the pole. If you don't have a table, spread out a picnic blanket and set your "table" on the ground. Use beautiful things from your garden as you decorate. Freshly picked flowers tucked in a watering can make a wonderful centerpiece. Use your imagination and have fun!

Garden Placemats

On pieces of white construction paper, draw a special garden for each of your guests. You could design a name garden for each friend. Choose a flower that starts with each letter of the person's name. My garden might have an **E**aster lily, **m**arigold, **i**ris, **l**ilac, **i**vy, and **e**vening primrose in it. See how that spells "Emilie"?

Some flowers have special meanings, so you could also design a hidden message garden on

the placemats. Decorate with morning glories to let your friends know they're special to you.

Whatever kind of garden you plant on your placemats, be sure to label the flowers. And don't forget to add plenty of greenery and a bug or two. Gardens always have ladybugs, earthworms, spiders, or praying mantises. Look at flower guides and seed catalogs to discover many kinds of flowers, and a sticker store can help you add the bugs!

Garden Napkin Rings

Cut napkin rings from cardboard tubes and then cover them with flowery fabric or contact paper. Use white napkins or give each guest a napkin that matches the flowers in her garden placemat.

Bug Bites

Plain round cookies—like sugar cookies or ginger snaps—for the bug bodies

Tubes of colored icing

Small candies like red-hots or mini M&Ms for spots, eyes, etc.

Licorice or fruit-flavored candy strings for legs, antennae, etc.

Use the icing and candies to turn cookies into a plateful of bugs to serve your guests. Don't forget the ants!

Or save the fun to share with your friends. Make or buy the cookies ahead of time and have your guests help you turn them into bugs.

Sunny Sandwiches

Sandwich bread

Apricot jam or orange marmalade

Carrot slices

Raisins

For each sandwich, spread two slices of bread with apricot jam. Cut off the crusts and use a biscuit cutter or round cookie cutter to cut the sandwiches into circles. Use carrot slices to make the rays of the sun. Add raisins for eyes and a sunny smile.

Garden Patch Cupcakes

One chocolate cupcake for each guest

Chocolate frosting

Crumbled chocolate sandwich cookies

Mint leaves

Thin drinking straws

Edible flowers or artifical flowers

Frost each cupcake with chocolate frosting. Then sprinkle each one with crumbled cookies to make dirt for your garden. Next cut the straws into 2- or 3-inch pieces and stand one in the middle of each cupcake. Then place a flower,

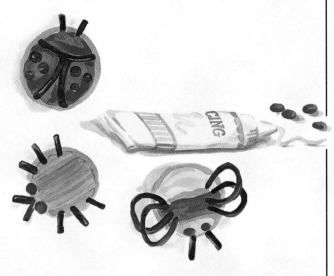

8

stem down, into each straw. If you use edible flowers, let your guests know that it's okay to eat the blossoms.

Raspberry Tea

A pot of tea, any flavor
(raspberry would be yummy!)

Fresh raspberries,
3–5 for each cup of tea

Brew your tea. Put raspberries in each cup before pouring in the tea.

More Fun!

SCAVENGER HUNT—Divide your guests into two groups and then send them out in your garden or yard to find certain items (a heart-shaped leaf, a moth, a packet of seeds, a watering can, etc.).

PIN THE BEE ON THE BLOSSOM—Paint a big piece of poster board with a very large, off-center rose. Draw winding stems, rosebuds, and leaves around the edges. Then, using a black marker, draw five or six bees onto yellow papers from self-stick pads. Make sure that at least part of the bee is on the sticky part! Then cut out the bees. At the party, blindfold each guest with a mask made of flowery material and have them take turns trying to stick the bee onto the large rose.

PAINTED FLOWERPOTS—Carefully wash 3½-inch clay pots (one for each guest plus one for you!) and let them dry. At the party, give your guests acrylic craft paints and brushes to decorate their pots, some newspapers to work on, and old T-shirts to wear during the fun. Plan to paint the flowerpots at the beginning of the tea so they can dry during the rest of the party. When your guests leave, be sure each one has a plastic bag of potting soil and a small packet of seeds. It will be a great reminder of your special garden tea party!

GARDEN SCARECROW—Every garden needs a scarecrow, and making one can be lots of fun. Either ask each guest to bring an old article of clothing or you provide all the clothes and accessories. You'll also need an old broomstick or wooden pole for the base and leaves, hay, or crumpled newspapers to stuff the clothes. Work together to decide on a name for your creation, and then let this "guest of honor" join you at the tea table before putting him or her to work in your garden.

Christine's Tea Party

Whatever you do,
do it with kindness and love.

THE BOOK OF 1 CORINTHIANS

Do you have a special friend—someone to laugh with and share secrets with? Someone to run with, play with, and just hang out with? Someone who knows what you're thinking before you say anything?

Well, one of my special friends is named Christine, and she just had a birthday. To celebrate that important day, we had a traditional and very elegant Victorian high tea. You know, the kind where tea is served in china cups and stirred with silver spoons. The kind of tea where very proper ladies wear white gloves and hold their little finger in the air when they sip their tea. It was the kind of pretty party every girl dreams of.

Here are some ideas for a party you could give for one of your special friends.

Invitations

First find some lovely white paper or printed-border note cards. Then use your fanciest handwriting to write invitations. Let your guests know when and where the party is and ask them to wear their dressiest clothes and to bring a pretty teacup to use.

An Elegant Table

For many years, hostesses have used a lovely white cloth made out of linen or crisp cotton for their fancy tea parties. You will also need white linen or cotton napkins. Silver napkin rings would be elegant, but you might want to tie satin ribbons around the napkins instead. Large gold or silver doilies make beautiful placemats. Then, for the centerpiece, you might use a fresh bouquet of roses and greenery, but daisies and baby breath are also nice. Pretty serving pieces like china plates, silver trays, and Grandma's teapot or cut-glass punchbowl would be special touches.

Serving Tea the Proper Way

Begin by asking each of your guests if she wants cream or sugar in her tea. Pour the cream into the cup first. Add sugar cubes next, one lump or two (or more) according to your guest's request. Finally, carefully pour the tea into the cup. Make sure you provide a spoon for stirring and a saucer to put under the cup. And always be sure to use your nicest manners at a tea party.

MENU: Angel Food Cake with Strawberries & Cream Cucumber Tea Sandwiches Chocolate-Dipped Strawberries Tea with Rosehips or Fruit Punch

Angel Food Cake with Strawberries and Cream

1 angel food cake (purchased or homemade)
2 pints of fresh strawberries
¼ cup of sugar
1 container of whipped topping

Wash the strawberries. Cut off the green stem and leaves. Then slice the strawberries. Sprinkle them with sugar and set them aside.

Next, with a long knife (and an adult's help), slice the cake horizontally twice so that you have three layers.

Now brush the loose crumbs off each layer and place the bottom layer on a pretty plate. Spread the top of the layer with whipped topping and then cover it with strawberry slices.

Place the second layer on top of the bottom one. Spread the top of this layer with whipped topping and strawberry slices.

Now place the top layer on the cake and frost the entire cake with the rest of the whipped topping.

Decorate the cake with the strawberries you have left. Store the cake in the refrigerator until it's time for tea.

Cucumber Tea Sandwiches

Cucumbers (how many cucumbers depends on how many people you will be serving)
White bread
Whipped cream cheese
Unsalted butter, softened
Salt

Peel the cucumbers and slice them very thin. Sprinkle the slices with salt and then put them on paper towels to drain. For each sandwich, spread a little bit of cream cheese on two slices of bread. Then layer the cucumber slices on one piece of bread, but don't stack them higher than ¼ inch. Now cut them into square tea sandwiches. (See how to make tea sandwiches on page 4.)

Chocolate-Dipped Strawberries

Whole fresh strawberries, washed and dried
Semisweet chocolate chips

Fill a small deep container (like a coffee cup) with chocolate chips and place it in the microwave. To melt the chocolate, heat it on high for 20 seconds, open the microwave and stir the chocolate, and then heat it again for 20 more seconds. Continue heating the chocolate at 20-second intervals until it is just melted. Then hold a strawberry by its broad top and dip the bottom part of the berry into the melted chocolate. Set the strawberry on wax paper to cool.

Continue dipping until you've dipped all the strawberries. Store the dipped berries in the refrigerator.

More Fun!

HATS FOR THE LADIES—
Decorate straw hats with silk flowers and beautiful ribbons. Wear your hats for tea—and be sure to pose for an elegant group picture.

DO-IT-YOURSELF CHINA—At a discount or thrift store, buy plain white or glass plates. Give one to each of your guests and then have everyone use glass or china paints (you can get them at craft stores) and tiny paintbrushes to decorate their plates with a sweet design.

BROKEN CUPS—Before the party, draw a pretty teacup for each guest. Make sure to include on each cup a special message like "Thanks for being my friend!" or "I'm so glad you came." Then cut each drawing into eight or ten pieces that aren't too easy to put back together. Put the pieces of each drawing into pretty envelopes (one set of teacup pieces per envelope) and give an envelope to each guest as she arrives. Then, sometime during the party, have your guests assemble their cups ("On your mark, get set, go!"). The first one who puts her broken cup back together is the winner.

TEATIME MEMORY TEASER—Bring out a tray on which you have put a number of well-known tea objects like a teacup, teabags, a tea strainer, a sugar bowl, milk, a lemon, and baked goodies. Bring out the tray and let your guests look at it for a full minute. Then take the tray away and give each person a pencil, a piece of paper, and three minutes to write down everything she saw on the tray. Remember, the more items you put on the tray, the more you tease the memory! Have a special gift ready for the person who remembers the greatest number of objects. You could let that person choose something from the tray.

Elizabeth's Pony Club Tea

There was not a day the boy did not pay me a visit, sometimes picking me out among the other horses, and giving me a bit of carrot, or something good....He always came with kind words and caresses, and of course I grew very fond of him.

ANNA SEWELL– *Black Beauty*

Do you ever picture yourself riding a chestnut mare through a field of wildflowers? Have you seen *National Velvet* or read *Black Beauty* so much that you've memorized parts? Do you ever dream of owning a horse and competing in a horse show, wearing either English jodhpurs or western chaps and boots?

My friend Elizabeth could answer yes to all these questions! I like horses, but Elizabeth is crazy about them. So we had a tea in her honor, and all of us were horses for a day. Try it yourself!

When your friends arrive, have each one write her favorite horse name on her name tag. That will be her name at the party.

Be sure to plan lots of games for your horse-guests. You can have relays and jumping contests, but the favorite will be the hurdles.

So, before the party, make some simple hurdles out of plastic pipes or lightweight wood posts or poles. Arrange the hurdles in your yard so that the horses will have a challenging course to run. Let the horse-guests practice with the hurdles low, but during the competition raise them each time the horses take a lap.

It's fun to have lots of awards ready, especially ones that look like the ribbons given at real horse shows. You can buy or make the ribbons before the party. You may even want to make a loving cup out of foil for the overall winner. You might invite a few adults to judge the competition and, more importantly, to take pictures of the events.

After the competition, let your horse-guests have a chance to cool down and relax a bit before tea. Give each of them a feed bucket (a plain white cardboard bucket or bag) to decorate with markers, stickers, and stamps. Remember that the best part of a horse's day is when the sweet grain comes. So when your horse-guests have to return to their own stables, be sure to put something sweet in their feed buckets.

Invitations

Remember how we made Garden Party invitations using folded pieces of paper? Follow the same steps (see page 6), but draw pony heads instead of suns or flowers. Then attach string or yarn as reins. In the invitations, ask each guest to bring her favorite model horse to add to the table decorations. And be sure to have your friends wear jeans or riding clothes.

A Winner's Circle Table

Cover your table with a green cloth. Make a Winner's Wreath Centerpiece out of tissue paper roses and lay a Saddle Placemat at every place. Slide each napkin through a Blue Ribbon Napkin Ring. Then, as each guest arrives, ask her to put her horse above her placemat at the table.

Winner's Wreath Centerpiece

Lots of red tissue paper, cut into 3" x 3" squares

Florist wire or green pipe cleaners

A Styrofoam wreath shaped like a horseshoe (If you can't find the right shape, cut a round or oval Styrofoam wreath to make a horseshoe.)

To make a paper rose, stack five squares of tissue paper together. Fold the stack back and forth and back and forth (like you're making a fan), making at least four folds. Pinch the folded stack in the middle and wrap a piece of wire around it, twisting the wire together below the paper to make a stem. One by one, pull apart the individual squares of tissue paper so that they form petals. Fluff these petals to make a pretty red rose. Then stick the wire stem into the Styrofoam. Make enough roses to cover the entire wreath.

Saddle Placemats

Draw saddles on large pieces of brown construction paper. Here's one kind of saddle you could use.

Blue Ribbon Napkin Rings

Make first-place ribbons out of blue construction paper. Then cut cardboard tubes into rings and cover them with the same blue paper. (You can make the rings out of construction paper, but cardboard ones are a little stronger.) Once you have the rings, glue a ribbon on top of each one.

MENU: Nosebag Oats-and-Raisin Cookies • Breadstick Horseshoes • Apple Slices • Baby Carrots • Mint Tea

Nosebag Oats-and-Raisin Cookies

1 cup of whole wheat flour

1 cup of oats

A little less than ¹/₂ cup of sugar

¹/₂ teaspoon of cinnamon

¹/₂ teaspoon of salt

¹/₂ teaspoon of baking powder

1 egg white

¹/₃ cup of light corn syrup

A little less than ¹/₄ cup of plain nonfat yogurt

1 teaspoon of vanilla extract

Some raisins

Preheat your oven to 375°. In a big bowl, mix together all the dry ingredients except the raisins. Then add the wet ingredients and mix well. Stir in some raisins (a few or a lot, depending on how you like your cookies). Then drop rounded teaspoons of dough onto a baking sheet. Bake for 10 minutes.

Breadstick Horseshoes

One can of ready-to-bake breadsticks
Parmesan cheese (if you want)

First cut each breadstick in half. Then, one by one, give each half a twist or two, curve it so that it's shaped like a horseshoe, and place it on a cookie sheet. If you want, sprinkle your horseshoes lightly with parmesan cheese. The breadsticks' wrapper will tell you how long to bake your horseshoes.

Books & Movies
FOR HORSE LOVERS

BOOKS

National Velvet by Enid Bagnold

If Wishes Were Horses, Leg Up for Lucinda, and *The Only Boy in the Ring* by Nancy Wright Grossman

Wild Mustang by Lynn Hall

Any horse story by Marguerite Henry, especially *Born to Trot* and *Misty of Chincoteague*

Smoky the Cow Horse by Will James

Somebody's Horse by Dorothy N. Morrison

Black Beauty by Anna Sewell

High Hurdles Series by Lauraine Snelling

The Black Stallion and other horse stories by Walter Farley

MOVIES

Black Beauty

The Black Stallion

Into the West

National Velvet

More Fun!

HORSIN' AROUND—Watch a good horse movie or read aloud parts of your favorite horse book. See "Books and Movies for Horse Lovers" for ideas.

STABLE TIME—Using cardboard boxes, paint, and other craft supplies, make a stable for your horses. Don't forget beautiful pastureland!

GIDDYUP—For an extra special treat, visit a stable or go on a trail ride.

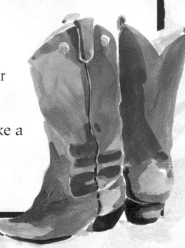

Tea for Little Women

The girls flew about, trying to make things comfortable, each in her own way. Meg arranged the tea table, Jo brought wood and set chairs, dropping, overturning, and clattering everything she touched, Beth trotted to and fro between parlor and kitchen, quiet and busy, while Amy gave directions to everyone.

Louisa May Alcott — *Little Women*

Little Women by Louisa May Alcott is my all-time favorite book. Have you read it? It's the story of four sisters who lived in the 1800s, and it's wonderful! Meg, Jo, Beth, and Amy lived in a world that's very different from ours, but they're girls who, like you and me, had their dreams, loved their family, and were not perfect! (Remember when Amy threw Jo's manuscript into the fire?) I love to imagine being Jo, telling stories, acting in plays with her three sisters, and, of course, enjoying tea. If your guests haven't read the book, watch some or all of the movie *Little Women* at the beginning of your tea.

Invitations

Choose pretty white or flowered note paper and write a formal invitation like this one:

Emilie Marie
requests the pleasure
of your company for a tea celebrating
<u>Little Women</u>,
by Louisa May Alcott

Saturday, June 16
between three and five o'clock
R.S.V.P.

Add your address before "R.S.V.P." and your phone number afterward, and of course use your name instead of mine!

Marmee's Surprise Table

The March family lived during the Civil War. Since Mr. March was away, Mrs. March (her four daughters called her "Marmee") didn't have much money. But the girls and their mother loved being together and they enjoyed what they did have.

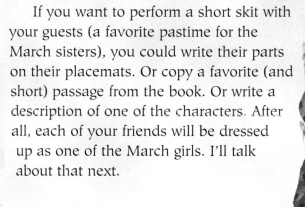

So, for your tea, start with a plain white tablecloth like the March girls used. See if you can find an older, slightly worn but still pretty one like the March family might have had. Put red and white flowers in a pretty vase and wrap ivy around it, letting some vines trail onto the table.

Old handkerchiefs make perfect napkins for your old-fashioned table. (If you can't get handkerchiefs, cut some squares of pretty cloth.) And here is an idea for your "open book" placemats.

If you want to perform a short skit with your guests (a favorite pastime for the March sisters), you could write their parts on their placemats. Or copy a favorite (and short) passage from the book. Or write a description of one of the characters. After all, each of your friends will be dressed up as one of the March girls. I'll talk about that next.

Jo's Dress-up Box

Before the party, fill a large box or chest with old-fashioned clothes (long skirts, high-necked blouses, cameo pins, high button shoes) and pretty hair ribbons and snoods (those little nets that hold a tucked-under ponytail at the back of your neck). When your guests arrive, have each one dress up like one of the March girls. You can either ask someone who knows how to braid to come and braid each guest's hair or you and your friends can practice on each other.

Since the March girls loved to act, you might ask each guest to take on the role of one of the sisters while you have your tea. (It's okay to have more than one motherly Meg, energetic Jo, peaceful Beth, or spirited Amy.) You and your guests could perform a scene from the book or make something up on your own.

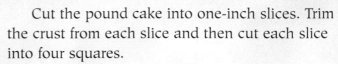

Pink and White Snowballs

Vanilla ice cream

Strawberry or peppermint ice cream

Flaked coconut

Line a small cookie sheet with wax paper. Then, using an ice cream scoop, make two ice cream balls—one vanilla and one strawberry or pepper-mint—for each guest. Roll each ball in coconut. Place the balls on the cookie sheet, cover the cookie sheet with foil, and freeze the snowballs until they are very firm.

Pretty Petit Fours

An already-cooked pound cake

2 cups of powdered sugar (or more if you make a lot of little cakes)

6 tablespoons of water

Food coloring

Tubes of decorating gel or, if you want, edible flowers

Cut the pound cake into one-inch slices. Trim the crust from each slice and then cut each slice into four squares.

To make the icing, add water—a tablespoon at a time—to the powdered sugar. Mix the sugar and water well after each tablespoon you pour in. Then add a couple drops of food coloring (red or yellow) and stir the icing until it is very smooth. You don't want any lumps!

Now place the small cake squares on a wire rack (the kind you use for cooling cakes and cookies) and drizzle some icing over each one. Be sure that each little piece of cake is thoroughly covered. (Make more icing if you need to.) Then let the icing dry.

Once the icing is dry, decorate your petit fours with gel or edible flowers.

20

Cherry Bonbons

Maraschino cherries with stems

Semisweet chocolate chips

Take the cherries out of the jar they come in and put them on paper towels so the liquid can drain off. Then fill a small deep container (like a coffee cup) with chocolate chips and place it in the microwave. To melt the chocolate, heat it on high for 20 seconds, open the microwave and stir the chocolate, and then heat it again for 20 more seconds. Continue heating the chocolate at 20-second intervals until it is just melted. Then hold the cherries by their stems and dip them in chocolate. Set the dipped cherries on wax paper. Chill these bonbons in the refrigerator.

More Fun!

MISS ALCOTT'S GIRLS—Read aloud chapter one of *Little Women* or, as I mentioned earlier, watch a movie version of this special book. (Two wonderful videos—one old, one new—are available.) Do this at the beginning of your party if your friends haven't read the book.

GUESS WHO?—If your friends know the story well, ask each one to choose a character from *Little Women*. Then play a "20 Questions" game. Have your friends take turns asking yes/no questions to each other (one person answers at a time) to try to figure out who each girl has chosen to be.

BOOK TRADE—Have each guest bring a favorite book to the tea. Give everyone a chance to tell why they brought their book. If you want, and if your guests know each other well enough, encourage them to trade books for a few weeks. Make sure people who trade books know who is borrowing theirs and when they will get it back. It's a good idea to have the owner of the book write her name, her phone number, and the date she's expecting it back on the inside front cover. Book owners may also want to have those who borrow their book sign their name and date on the inside back cover. You and your guests might even decide to make a certain day each month "Book Trading Day." It might be fun to see which book has the most signatures at the end of the year.

SECRET TREASURE JOURNAL—Give each of your guests 16 sheets of lined paper (the kind with the holes) and three pieces of pretty ribbon. Tie the ribbon through the holes to make a secret treasure journal. Then let your friends decorate the cover with stickers, stamps and marking pens. Each of your friends will now have something to write their dreams and memories in.

A Musical Tea Party

I love music—and I hope you do, too. I love to listen to music, to sing to music, to dance to music, and to make music. I've been learning to play the cello, and when I practice I think about someday wearing a long black dress and playing in a symphony orchestra. I would love to join with other musicians to play beautiful music. At a musical tea, your friends can join you in singing, playing, and celebrating beautiful, joyful music.

Invitations

Call your friends together with a song! First find the sheet music to a song you like. Then copy a few bars of the melody onto the front of the first invitation. Copy the next few bars onto the next invitation. Do you see the pattern? Keep working until the front of each invitation has part of the song on it. Then you can write details about the party inside. Invite your guests to wear fancy clothes like people wear to a symphony concert. Ask them to bring their invitations and any small musical instruments they have to the party. When your friends arrive, they can piece together the invitation song and you can all sing it.

Coming through pale fawn fluff at about half-past eleven on a very sunny morning, it seemed to Pooh to be one of the very best songs he had ever sung. So he went on singing it.

A.A. MILNE – *The House at Pooh Corner*

An Onstage Table

Cover your table with a red cloth. Using a real musical instrument or two, start to create your centerpiece. Tuck a few pieces of sheet music around and under the instruments. For a classy touch, add a candle in a tall holder or a few carnations in a vase. Then set each place with a Noteworthy Names Placemat and use Tambourine Napkin Rings for your napkins. Choose some music to play in the background and the symphony of fun can begin!

Noteworthy Names Placemats

White construction paper

A ruler

A pencil

A black marker

Someone who knows how to read music

Draw a large musical staff (five horizontal and parallel lines) on each piece of white construction paper. Then set each guest's name to music. My placemat might look like this:

Tambourine Napkin Rings

First cut cardboard tubes into rings and paint them black or silver. Then use a hole punch to make four holes on both edges of each ring. Lace a thin black ribbon (about 6 inches long) through each hole and use it to tie jingle bells to the napkin rings. Then slide a red or white napkin through each tambourine.

EM-I-LIE MA-RIE

Piano Key Sandwiches

Pumpernickel bread
White bread
Softened butter
Apple butter
Chopped apple
Chopped walnuts
Whipped cream cheese
A small can of crushed pineapple (drain the juice)

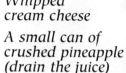

First make the dark key sandwiches. Spread apple butter on two slices of pumpernickel bread. Then add some apple pieces and chopped walnuts. Cut each sandwich into four rectangular tea sandwiches.

To make the white key sandwiches, mix two tablespoons of pineapple into ½ cup of the whipped cream cheese. Spread the cream cheese mix between two slices of white bread. Slice these into four rectangular tea sandwiches.

When you serve your special sandwiches, try arranging them on a platter so they look like the black and white keys on a piano.

Drum Cupcakes

One cupcake for every guest
Frosting (light chocolate would be nice)
Tubes of red decorative icing
Small candies like red-hots or mini M&Ms
Some thin pretzel sticks

Frost your cupcakes. Be sure to cover the sides as well as the top. Then use the decorative icing and the pieces of candy to turn each cupcake into a little drum (see the picture for one way to do it). The last step is to lay two thin pretzel sticks on top. They're your drumsticks!

Flute Cookies

Long, tube-shaped cookies (store-bought)
A tube of decorative icing

Add dots of decorative icing as finger holes on your "flutes."

24

More Fun!

CENTER STAGE—Have a recital. Ask guests who play an instrument or who can sing to perform at your tea party.

BE A SONGWRITER—Choose a tune you already know but make up some new words for it. Maybe you could write a song about tea!

SING-A-LONG TIME—Have a group sing-a-long. You can ask someone to play the guitar or the piano, or you might even rent a karaoke machine.

GUESS WHO'S HUMMING—Ask your guests to stand in a circle. The person who is "It" stands blindfolded in the center. As your friends walk slowly around "It," they sing a song. When "It" says, "Stop!" the people in the circle stop moving, but they keep singing. "It" then points to one of the guests, and everyone else immediately stops singing. The person to whom "It" pointed starts to hum the song, and "It" tries to guess who is humming. If "It" guesses correctly, she and the one humming trade places. If "It" doesn't guess who was humming, she tries again. Let each of your friends have a chance to be "It." (This game works best if your guests know each other pretty well.)

TOP TUNES—It's always fun to share our favorite music, and your tea party is a great time for that. You can have your guests bring a favorite cassette tape or CD. Then, while you're all enjoying tea, each of your friends could play their favorite song for the rest of the group.

MUSIC PANTOMIME—This game is a lot like "Simon Says," but this time Simon is the conductor of the orchestra. Simon begins by pretending to play a certain musical instrument, and everyone in the orchestra follows Simon's example. At any time, Conductor Simon can change the instrument she's playing. When she says, "Simon says, 'Play a drum,'" others should follow. But when she says, "Play a trombone," the orchestra members who respond are out of the game.

Tea with Grammy

Aren't grandmothers wonderful? They're a little bit of mother, a little bit of teacher, and a little bit of best friend all in one. They often have special stories, special treats, and special talents to share. I love to hear my grammy talk about when she was a girl and when my mom was a girl. I love my grammy's homemade pickles and baking-soda biscuits and canned peaches. And it's always fun to sit and stitch and, of course, share a cup of tea with her.

Here's a tea to prepare and share with your grandmother (or another special older adult). If you don't have a grandmother or she lives far away, have an "adopt a Grandma" tea and invite a special older person you know and want to get to know better.

Invitations

One thing that makes this tea extra fun is that you and your grammy (or special guest) prepare it together. So, on a pretty piece of paper, tell your guest of honor that you're glad she's part of your life. Then invite her to share in a tea party with you from start to finish! If you can, deliver your invitation in person with a big hug and a pretty flower. While you're together, choose a day to cook, decorate, and share tea. Mark the day on both your calendars with a big red heart.

A Cozy Table

Cover your table with a family quilt. Make a centerpiece out of framed family photos or other family treasures. Then add Handwoven Placemats and napkins in Forget-Me-Not Rings.

Handwoven Placemats

For each placemat, choose two different colors of construction paper. (You might want to choose two colors that match the quilt you'll be using as a tablecloth.) Fold one sheet of paper in half like the picture shows. Using a ruler and a pencil, make between five and ten evenly spaced marks along the folded edge. At each mark, use your scissors to cut straight in from each notch, stopping about an inch before you get to the other edge of the folded paper. Next cut the other piece of paper along the short side into 1-inch strips. Now weave these strips of paper through the slits in the first sheet of paper (look at the picture again). When you've finished weaving, glue down any loose ends.

Forget-Me-Not Napkin Rings

Forget-me-nots are beautiful blue flowers that grow on delicate thin stalks, and those stems make them perfect for shaping into little wreaths! Find some silk forget-me-nots at a craft store. (Other small flowers or ivy can work, too.) You'll need several stalks for each napkin ring. Hold three or four stalks together and make a circle out of them. Then use floral wire to hold the wreath together.

For a sweet touch, hide a handwritten note between the napkin and the ring. A message of love like "No one could ever take your place" or "You are so special to me" would be perfect.

FOLD

MENU: Grammy's Old-fashioned Scones • Cream
Toppings or Preserves and Jams • Kidstuff
Nutty-Raisin Sandwiches • Heirloom Treasures • Spiced Tea

Grammy's Old-fashioned Scones

2 cups of flour

1 tablespoon of baking powder

2 tablespoons of sugar

½ teaspoon of salt

6 tablespoons of butter

½ cup of buttermilk

1 lightly beaten egg

Mix together all the dry ingredients. Then use a pastry cutter or two knives to cut in 6 tablespoons of butter until mixture resembles coarse cornmeal. (Grammy will know how to do that!) Make a well in the center of your dough and pour in the buttermilk. Stir until the dough clings together and is a bit sticky. (Be careful not to stir too much. You don't want the scones to be tough.)

Now put the dough on a floured surface and flatten it into a circle that's 1 ½ inches thick and between six and eight inches across. Working quickly, cut the dough into triangles like pieces of a pie or use a large round biscuit cutter to cut it into circles.

Put your triangles or circles on an ungreased cookie sheet. Make sure that the sides of the scones don't touch each other. Then brush some of the lightly beaten egg on top so that your scones will be a shiny, beautiful brown.

Bake at 425° for 10–20 minutes until the pastries are light brown. Serve your scones with some special creams (you'll find two recipes following, but in a pinch you can buy whipped topping at the store) or your favorite preserves and jams (red raspberry or strawberry are nice).

Sue's Creme Fraiche

1 cup of heavy cream

1 tablespoon of buttermilk

Pour the cream and the buttermilk into a saucepan and stir them together on your stove. Have the burner set at a medium heat. Heat the mixture just until the chill is off (that's about 90° if you have a kitchen thermometer). Once the chill is off, pour the mixture into a glass jar, cover it lightly with a piece of

28

waxed paper, and let it sit in a warm place (65°-70°) to thicken. It takes between 12 and 20 hours. Once it's thick, replace the wax paper with plastic wrap or a tight-fitting lid and refrigerate your creme fraiche for at least 6 hours. (It will last for about two weeks if you keep it in the refrigerator.) You might want to whip your creme to make it thicker or add a little sugar to make it sweet.

Mock Devonshire Cream

½ cup of heavy cream or 8 ounces of softened cream cheese

2 tablespoons of confectioners' sugar

½ cup of sour cream

In a chilled bowl, beat the cream until medium-stiff peaks form. Add the sugar during the last few minutes of beating. (If you use cream cheese, just stir it and the sugar together.) Fold (that's a gentler movement than stirring) in the sour cream and blend. Makes 1½ cups.

Kidstuff Nutty-Raisin Sandwiches

Raisin bread

Soft butter

Whipped cream cheese

Chopped pecans

For each sandwich, spread two slices of raisin bread with a little bit of butter. Then spread on some cream cheese. Sprinkle chopped pecans on top of the cream cheese and close the sandwich. Cut off the crusts and then use small cookie cutters to cut your sandwiches into fancy shapes.

Heirloom Treasures

Dried apricots

White melting chocolate (from the baking section at the grocery store)

Small silver baking cups

Cooking spray

To melt the chocolate, read and follow the directions on the package. Spray the inside of each baking cup lightly with cooking spray. Dip half of each apricot in chocolate. Swirl each apricot around so it gets a nice, thick coating of chocolate. Place each dipped apricot—chocolate side down—in a silver baking cup. Refrigerate your yummy treasures.

Spiced Tea Mix

1 cup of dry instant tea (I like decaffeinated)
2 cups of dry powdered orange drink
3 cups of sugar
½ cup of red-hots
1 teaspoon of ground cinnamon
½ teaspoon of powdered cloves
1 package (about 1 cup) of lemonade mix

Stir together all ingredients and place the mixture in a covered container. When it's time to make the tea, use one heaping tablespoon for each cup of hot water. Stir it well and then enjoy.

More Fun!

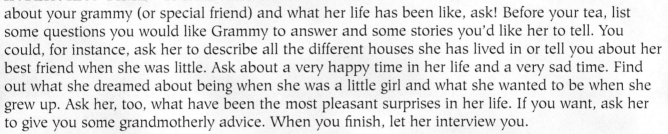

INTERVIEW TIME—To learn more about your grammy (or special friend) and what her life has been like, ask! Before your tea, list some questions you would like Grammy to answer and some stories you'd like her to tell. You could, for instance, ask her to describe all the different houses she has lived in or tell you about her best friend when she was little. Ask about a very happy time in her life and a very sad time. Find out what she dreamed about being when she was a little girl and what she wanted to be when she grew up. Ask her, too, what have been the most pleasant surprises in her life. If you want, ask her to give you some grandmotherly advice. When you finish, let her interview you.

TOGETHER CRAFT—Choose an activity—like quilting, needlepoint, canning, or making a favorite family food—that your grammy can teach you. Or maybe you can teach Grammy how to do a craft—like stamping or making friendship bracelets—that you enjoy.

FAMILY PICTURES—Look at family photo albums together and talk about the pictures. Turn this fun into a treasure hunt by looking for things like the strangest clothes, the worst hairstyle, the cutest baby, and the most adorable guy. Choose your own interesting things to find!

FAVORITE SONGS—Ask Grammy to teach you her favorite childhood song and then teach her one of your favorites. (Grammies are also great for favorite dances!)

A SECRET "I LOVE YOU"—Come up with a special word, symbol, hand gesture, or code that will have a secret meaning just for you and your grammy. Maybe squeezing her hand three times will mean "I love you" or "RILY" will stand for "Remember I Love You."

I hope you've enjoyed having tea with me. It's been fun to share some of my ideas for special teatimes with you. You could also plan a tea celebrating your favorite color or your favorite book—from *Winnie-the-Pooh* to *Matilda*. You could learn about the traditions of another country and plan a tea that shows what you learn. How about a "Moonlight Lawn Tea" or a "Teddy Bear Tea"? I bet you have ideas of your own. The possibilities are endless. Just dream and then have fun as you share tea!

Recipes and Crafts

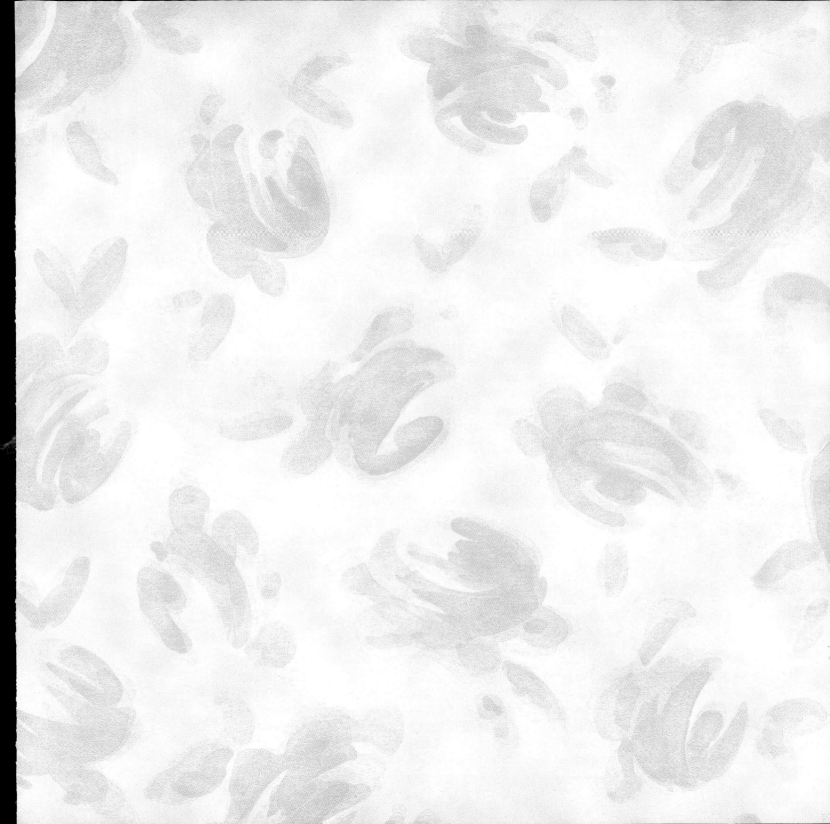